Coping™

COPING WITH
FAKE NEWS AND DISINFORMATION

Devlin Smith

Published in 2020 by The Rosen Publishing Group, Inc.
29 East 21st Street, New York, NY 10010

Copyright © 2020 by The Rosen Publishing Group, Inc.

First Edition

All rights reserved. No part of this book may be reproduced in any form without permission in writing from the publisher, except by a reviewer.

Library of Congress Cataloging-in-Publication Data

Names: Smith, Devlin.
Title: Coping with fake news and disinformation / Devlin Smith.
Description: New York : Rosen Publishing, 2020. | Series: Coping | Includes bibliographical references and index.
Identifiers: LCCN 2019009353| ISBN 9781725341203 (library bound) | ISBN 9781725341197 (pbk.)
Subjects: LCSH: Media literacy—Juvenile literature. | Fake news—Juvenile literature.
Classification: LCC P96.M4 .S64 2019 | DDC 070.4/3—dc23
LC record available at https://lccn.loc.gov/2019009353

Manufactured in China

On the cover: Thanks to connected devices, we now have constant access to information. Accuracy and validity aren't guaranteed so it's important to develop tools to judge that information.

Some of the images in this book illustrate individuals who are models. The depictions do not imply actual situations or events.

CONTENTS

INTRODUCTION **4**

CHAPTER ONE
A Free Press **7**

CHAPTER TWO
Making the News **22**

CHAPTER THREE
Faking the News **37**

CHAPTER FOUR
Finding the Truth **53**

CHAPTER FIVE
Information Overload **67**

CHAPTER SIX
Consuming the News **80**

GLOSSARY   99

FOR MORE INFORMATION   101

FOR FURTHER READING   104

BIBLIOGRAPHY   105

INDEX   108

INTRODUCTION

When Apple released iOS 12 in September 2018, the update included the new feature Screen Time. It provides users with reports on the amount of time they spend on their phones and what they are doing, like using apps or going online. Digital Wellbeing was introduced for Android devices in November 2018 and provides similar information to users about how they interact with their phones.

According to data reported by Nielsen in a July 2018 study, Americans spent an average of three hours and forty-eight minutes a day on digital media in the first quarter of 2018, with most of that time spent using apps to go online with their smartphones. Released by the Canadian Internet Registration Authority (CIRA) in March 2018, "Canada's Internet Factbook 2018" revealed that 74 percent of Canadians spend at least three to four hours a day online; 14 percent spend more than eight hours a day online.

Online we shop, connect with family and friends, watch videos, listen to music, do research, and get news. The information and news we find online, though, may not be accurate. Stories from long-established media brands, like national magazines and local newspapers, blogs, message boards, and social media channels, find their ways into our feeds, presenting information that could be true, inaccurate, false, or fabricated.

With features like iOS Screen Time and Android Digital Wellbeing, smartphone users can better understand their digital habits, including the amount of time they spend online.

Judging the quality of the information and news we find online can be a challenge, as Christian Picciolini, a reformed neo-Nazi and peace advocate, described for the CNN special report "Spreading Hate: The Dark Side of the Internet." "There's so much misinformation out there, it's tough to distinguish what's real, what's fake, what's propaganda, what's parody, and it's confusing for young people who are searching for an answer," he said in the special.

If it aligns with our beliefs and confirms our biases, we may spread fake news and misinformation across our social networks. Our shares can lead to more shares, and that bad information will continue to spread. Even if our followers are limited to close family and friends, what we share can have an influence. For those with larger followings, their posts can have even more of an impact. Deema Al Asaid, a social media influencer, shared the concerns she has about what she posts in the 2017 documentary *Follow Me*:

> *The more followers I have, the more responsibility I feel about what I share on social media because it's such a huge responsibility, so I try to take it seriously, and I hope that all the people who are actually influencers and have people following them, they take this really seriously, because the power of social media, or saying anything on social media, is crazy.*

Whether your social network includes millions or just hundreds of followers, you can take action to limit the spread of fake news and disinformation. You can explore the positive and negative impacts news media can have, learn how to judge the validity of the information you find online, and discover resources to help you develop better news judgment.

A Free Press

CHAPTER ONE

Johannes Gutenberg changed the world. Prior to Gutenberg's invention of the printing press in the mid-fifteenth century, the reproduction of books, pamphlets, and other media was most often done by hand. Books were in short supply, and with few books, few people were able to read. At the time of the printing press's invention, just 30 percent of Europeans were literate, according to data shared by Tatiana Schlossberg in an article that appeared on McSweeney's Internet Tendency on February 7, 2011.

The automation provided by Gutenberg's printing press led to the release of more books, pamphlets, and other media. With words and information more readily available, more people were able to learn to read. Three centuries after the printing press's invention, the US Constitution was signed, and 60 percent of the new country's

Johannes Gutenberg's invention of the printing press in the mid-fifteenth century led to vast increases in literacy and in the production of books, pamphlets, and other print media.

free adult population was literate, according to data shared by Schlossberg. In 2017, the UNESCO (United Nations Educational, Scientific and Cultural Organization) Institute for Statistics (UIS) reported that 99 percent of adults in Europe and North America were literate; the global adult literacy rate was 86 percent.

Gutenberg's invention laid the groundwork for generations of technologies that would continue to improve access to information, including typewriters, copy machines, and computers. The printing press also enabled the development of journalistic print media—later to include radio, television, and the internet—that collectively became known as "the press."

Controlling the Press

When technologies emerge, governments often debate what regulations should be enacted, determining who can use the new technology, how the new technology can be used, and when the new technology can be used. Cars, for example, are heavily regulated.

All drivers need to be licensed. To get your driver's license, you must reach a minimum age, complete training, and pass tests. Once you have your license, you must obey the laws of the road and renew your license every few years. Speed limits are set to restrict how fast you can drive your car. Drivers and passengers must wear seatbelts. Infants and small children must ride in car seats or in booster seats. Car owners are also responsible for maintaining their vehicles for road safety.

Public safety informs regulations placed on cars. Throughout history, though, governments have sought to regulate the press in order to control information that is spread, including limiting or eliminating the spread of information that is critical of the government.

In the seventeenth century, one way the press in the United Kingdom—and later the British colonies in North America—was regulated was through licensing. In accordance with the Licensing Act, before any book or pamphlet could be printed, it had to first be registered with the Stationers' Company, a government-approved guild of printers. (The Stationers' Company is still in existence today, with over nine hundred members who represent press organizations, as well as paper, print, publishing, and office products companies.) By requiring registration, the law was, as detailed in Karen Nipps's 2014 article in the *Library Quarterly*, "giving the king his 'royal prerogative'—and by extension, giving the Stationers the ultimate say in what got printed and what did not."

The Licensing Act—which would go through periods of renewal and lapse before lapsing for good in 1697—did not eliminate press freedom in the United Kingdom, but it did limit it. Preventing someone from writing or saying something in advance is known as "prior restraint." Prior restraint was an issue of debate for the Founding Fathers as

A Free Press

Freedom of the Student Press

The First Amendment of the US Constitution and court rulings have affirmed the rights of professional journalists and media. High school journalists may not enjoy the same level of press freedom as their professional, adult counterparts.

The 1988 Supreme Court case *Hazelwood School District v. Kuhlmeier* involved a high school paper in St. Louis, Missouri, challenging censorship by the school's principal. Because the paper was sponsored by the school, the Supreme Court ruled the students' free speech rights were not violated when the principal censored their stories.

Under this ruling, public school officials can censor student articles they deem inappropriate. The ruling, though, applies only to school newspapers that serve as a "limited forum," meaning that the paper's content is controlled by school officials instead of by the students, as explained on the website of the Administrative Office of the US Courts, uscourts.gov.

If the public school paper is a forum for student expression, with students making the content decisions as opposed to advisers, student journalists will have stronger First Amendment protection, according to the Student Press Law Center (SPLC), a Washington, DC–based organization that provides advocacy and education to student journalists and their advisers. Public school student journalists can further protect

Students on the Hazelwood East High School newspaper, including editor Tammy Hawkins (*above*), challenged censorship in a case that went all the way to the US Supreme Court.

their work through ethical writing and reporting, including checking all facts and ensuring the work is not libelous.

Students journalists at private schools may have fewer First Amendment protections than students in public schools do, depending on where the school is located. Private high school and college students in California do have First Amendment protections thanks to the Leonard Law, passed in 1992. For students in other states, the SPLC has recommendations on how to fight against press censorship, including suggesting policy changes to administrators or even establishing an independent publication not controlled by your school.

they tackled freedom of the press and freedom of speech in the US Constitution.

If something the government found objectionable did manage to be licensed and published, laws were enacted that could be used to limit the press after the fact. Victoria Gardner, lecturer in modern British history at the University of Manchester, detailed this further press regulation in a *History Today* article in February 2013:

Prosecutions could be brought successfully for treason, seditious libel and blasphemy. Prosecutions for libel had always been scattershot, but the threat of prison was enough to quieten all but the hardiest of radicals when only the fact of a libel and criminal intent had to be established.

Press in the Americas

North America's first printing press arrived in the Massachusetts Bay colony in 1638. Colonial governments enforced the British press licensing law. With the final lapse of the Licensing Act in the late seventeenth century, local colonial governments debated implementing their own licensing laws to further limit the press, as Robert W. T. Martin detailed in *The Free and Open Press: The Founding of American Democratic Press Liberty, 1640–1800*:

> *By 1700, men debated in sworn depositions whether or not licensing was a "new thing," and soon there were "numerous" controversial but unlicensed pamphlets. In 1704, Boston's first (sustained) newspaper appeared; the second arrived in 1719. Finally, in 1721, Governor Samuel Shute*

appealed to the Massachusetts General Court for a licensing law, thus conceding that, though his royal instructions had not changed, they had become irrelevant. The House refused to enact any such law, noting "the innumerable inconveniences and dangerous Circumstances the People might Labour under" if the governor were to control the press.

The colonial American press may have been free from licensing restrictions in the eighteenth century, but they could still have their ability to publish limited by libel laws. One of America's best-known libel trials occurred decades before the country gained its independence. The case of *Crown v. John Peter Zenger* was heard in 1735. Upset with the critical coverage he was receiving in the *New-York Weekly Journal*, New York governor William Cosby and his administration sought to charge not the newspaper's editors with seditious libel—publishing malicious content about the government—but to instead charge John Peter Zenger, the paper's printer, in an effort to shut the paper down. The validity of the statements made in the paper did not matter, the question of the case was whether Zenger published those statements or not.

Representatives of the British colonial government burn copies of John Peter Zenger's *New-York Weekly Journal*, which faced a seditious libel charge for publishing criticisms of local officials.

Zenger won his case and was found not guilty by a jury and returned to printing. The Historical Society of the New York Courts summarized the lasting legacy of this case, not just on press freedom but also on the judicial system in the United States:

It is important to note that the Zenger case did not establish legal precedent in seditious libel or freedom of the press. Rather, it influenced how people thought about these subjects and led, many decades later, to the protections embodied in the United States Constitution, the Bill of Rights and the Sedition Act of 1798. The Zenger case demonstrated the growing independence of the professional Bar and reinforced the role of the jury as a curb on executive power.

The US Constitution was shaped by this history with the Founding Fathers valuing the flow of information and the ability of citizens to criticize their government, but also seeing value in placing some limits on the press. From this came the First Amendment of the US Constitution, ratified in 1791, which states, "Congress shall make no law respecting an establishment of religion, or prohibiting the free exercise thereof; or abridging the freedom of speech, or of the press; or the right of the people peaceably to assemble, and to petition the government for a redress of grievances."

Though establishing an independent press in the United States—meaning a press not operated or controlled by the government—the First Amendment did not protect the press in the United States from any and all limitations. The first restriction came with the Sedition Act of 1798, which made it illegal to write or say something false, scandalous, or malicious against the government. People were jailed for violating the act before it expired in 1801.

Press freedom is guaranteed in both the US Constitution and Canadian Charter of Rights and Freedoms, but that freedom is not without restrictions, including laws against libel and slander.

Members of the press are prohibited from writing (libel) or saying (slander) anything knowingly false about a person and can be sued for the false statements they report. The government can request a story not be published or aired if it threatens national security. Journalists can be asked to turn over their notes or reveal their sources if they have information that could impact national security or public safety, such as witnessing a crime while reporting a story.

Publications can challenge these requests in court, citing the First Amendment protection of the press, a protection few other occupations enjoy in the United States, as former *Las Vegas Review-Journal* business reporter Jennifer Robison expressed in the 2017 documentary *Nobody Speak: Trials of the Free Press*: "Reporting is the only job specifically listed in the Bill of Rights as protected, it is a sacred public trust, a vital civic function, truly the fourth estate, the watchdog over the powerful. Without good, strong journalism, you don't have a healthy democracy."

In Canada, Section 2 of the Canadian Charter of Rights and Freedoms, enacted in 1982, established that country's independent press. It reads, "Everyone has the following fundamental freedoms: a. freedom of conscience and religion; b. freedom of thought, belief, opinion and expression, including freedom of the press and

Coping with Fake News and Disinformation

Demonstrators gather outside the offices of the *New York Times* to protest the Trump administration's decision to deny media outlets, including the *Times*, access to an off-camera briefing.

other media of communication; c. freedom of peaceful assembly; and d. freedom of association."

Like their counterparts in the United States, Canadian journalists can also be subject to libel or slander complaints and may be required by the government to turn over their reporting notes or reveal their sources. Freedom House, an independent watchdog organization that monitors and reports on challenges to freedom around the world, rated the press in both the United States and Canada as "free" in its "Freedom of the Press 2017" report. The organization reported just 13 percent of the world's population lived in countries with a free press.

CHAPTER TWO

Making the News

As the United States expanded west throughout the nineteenth century, eventually stretching from the Atlantic coast to the Pacific, so, too, did the country's press grow. Newspapers provided the growing nation's people with information on the wars, discoveries, and tragedies that would define their time in history.

Like the media of today, nineteenth-century newspapers were covering current events but also featuring in-depth reporting on major societal issues. One example was the undercover reporting done by Elizabeth Cochrane Seaman (using her pen name Nellie Bly) at the New York State Lunatic Asylum on Blackwell's Island in New York. Cochrane posed as a patient to gather firsthand accounts of the mistreatment experienced by patients at the facility. Her reporting, which appeared in Joseph Pulitzer's *New York World*

22

Making the News

> Under the pen name Nellie Bly, undercover reporter Elizabeth Cochrane Seaman exposed abusive treatment of patients in a lunatic asylum for the *New York World* newspaper.

newspaper in 1887, helped lead to major reforms at the asylum.

While providing American readers with news, information, and opinion in their papers, many publishers also ran incredibly successful businesses. Publishers like Pulitzer and William Randolph Hearst gained power and built fortunes operating papers in cities throughout the United States. Filling their pages with sensational stories of local crime and international strife, these publishers were able to influence government policy and sell a lot of newspapers. This type of journalism came to be

23

known as "yellow journalism," named for the character in a popular comic strip that ran first in Pulitzer's *New York World* and then in Hearst's *New York Journal*.

Calling for War

After nearly four hundred years of Spanish colonial rule, Cubans were fighting for their independence

Newspapers published by William Randolph Hearst and Joseph Pulitzer sometimes printed false accounts of the Cuban revolution to encourage the US government to enter the war.

in the late 1800s. Many in the United States backed this growing revolution, including Pulitzer and Hearst, as noted in a US Department of State Office of the Historian article: "Hearst and Pulitzer devoted more and more attention to the Cuban struggle for independence, at times accentuating the harshness of Spanish rule or the nobility of the revolutionaries, and occasionally printing rousing stories that proved to be false. This sort of coverage, complete with bold headlines and creative drawings of events, sold a lot of papers for both publishers."

The newspapers featured articles about what was occurring in Cuba, even if they didn't always have reporters on the ground to cover the events, as Clifford Krauss described in a 1998 *New York Times* article: "Though it did not have a correspondent on the ground as the Cuban rebellion heated up in 1895, the Hearst paper shamelessly attached Havana datelines to bylined stories creatively manufactured by rewrite men back in New York who interviewed exiled Cuban supporters of the revolt."

The newspapers were open in their support of the Cuban revolutionaries, as were their reporters. As Krauss detailed, reporters would bring medicine and rum to gain access to fighters. One reporter helped a teenager accused of incitement break out of jail and escape to the United States. Hearst sent a ceremonial sword with a diamond-studded ivory handle to the commander of the rebels, General Maximo Gomez.

The US government was not yet convinced to get involved and wage war on Spain. The government did, however, display its military might in the region. The battleship *Maine* was sent to Havana as part of this effort. On February 15, 1898, the battleship sunk in the Havana harbor following an explosion. More than 225 Americans were killed. Debate flourished over the cause of the explosion. The newspapers quickly placed the blame on Spain, as Christopher Woolf reported for a December 2016 radio story on PRI's *The World*: "The cause was never discovered. But the yellow press jumped to the conclusion that the Spanish did it deliberately. 'Remember the Maine' became the slogan of the yellow press, driving public opinion toward war."

Following the *Maine*'s sinking, the United States entered into the Spanish-American War and won. Spain gave up control over Cuba. The United States gained sovereignty over Guam, Puerto Rico, and the Philippines.

Multiple factors influenced the US government's decision to go to war with Spain, including a growing national interest in overseas expansion and the press coverage of the day. According to the State Department's Office of the Historian:

MAINE EXPLOSION CAUSED BY BOMB OR TORPEDO?

Capt. Sigsbee and Consul-General Lee Are in Doubt---The World Has Sent a Special Tug, With Submarine Divers, to Havana to Find Out---Lee Asks for an Immediate Court of Inquiry---Capt. Sigsbee's Suspicions.

I. SIGSBEE, IN A SUPPRESSED DESPATCH TO THE STATE DEPARTMENT, SAYS THE ACCIDENT WAS MADE POSSIBLE BY AN ENEMY.

E. C. Pendleton, Just Arrived from Havana, Says He Overheard Talk There of a Plot to Blow Up the Ship---Capt Zalinski, the Dynamite Expert, and Other Experts Report to The World that the Wreck Was Not Accidental---Washington Officials Ready for Vigorous Action if Spanish Responsibility Can Be Shown---Divers to Be Sent Down to Make Careful Examinations.

The New York World a day after

who had been Populists and those who became Progressives — clamored for the United States to rescue the Cuban people from the Spanish malefactors.

President William McKinley and the conservative Republican leaders in Congress reluctantly gave way before this pressure. Senator Henry Cabot Lodge warned McKinley, "If the war in Cuba drags on through the summer with nothing done we [the Republican party] shall go down in the greatest defeat ever known."

Already, in November 1897, Spain, at the urging of President McKinley, had granted

Though the cause was never discovered, American newspapers blamed the sinking of the US battleship *Maine* on Spanish forces, coverage that propelled the United States to wage war.

Yellow journalism of this period is significant to the history of U.S. foreign relations in that its centrality to the history of the Spanish-American War shows that the press had the power to capture the attention of a large readership and to influence public reaction to international events. The dramatic style of yellow journalism contributed to creating public support for the Spanish-American War, a war that would ultimately expand the global reach of the United States.

Inciting Prejudice and Violence

Pulitzer and Hearst were far from the first people to spread exaggerated or false stories for political purposes, as Jacob Soll reported in an article for Politico:

Fake news is not a new phenomenon. It has been around since news became a concept 500 years ago with the invention of print—a lot longer, in fact, than verified, "objective" news, which emerged in force a little more than a century ago. From the start, fake news has tended to be sensationalist and extreme, designed to inflame passions and prejudices. And it has often provoked violence.

Soll recounted several examples from history in his article, the oldest dating back to the fifteenth century. A toddler went missing in Trent, Italy, and a preacher blamed members of the local Jewish community for the disappearance. He claimed that the child was murdered and his blood drained and drunk as part of a Passover celebration. The account spread, leading to the arrest and torture of members of Trent's Jewish community. According to Soll's reporting, fifteen people were found guilty of the child's murder and were burned at the stake.

During the American Revolution, false reports were spread to increase support for the fight for independence, according to Soll's report. News was spread that the United Kingdom had enlisted Native Americans and foreign soldiers to join its fight against the American revolutionaries. In the 1800s, before the start of the Civil War, stories were spread about slave uprisings and crimes committed by slaves to turn public opinion against African Americans, with violent results.

An exhibit at the Boone History & Culture Center in Columbia, Missouri, shared more historical examples of rumors, hoaxes, and false news reports.

"The History of Fake News (and the Importance of the World's Oldest School of Journalism)" ran from July 2018 through January 2019 at the center, which is located near the University of Missouri, home to one of the world's first journalism schools. The exhibit included headlines boasting that animals and dinosaurs had been discovered on the moon, photographs believed to have proved the existence of fairies, and even Orson Welles's 1938 radio play

In 1938, Orson Welles and his Mercury Theater produced the radio play *War of the Worlds.* Panicked listeners believed they were hearing live reports of an actual alien invasion.

War of the Worlds, which listeners believed to be an actual news report of an alien invasion.

In addition to providing historical examples of what is now referred to as fake news, exhibit organizers highlighted what they felt was the solution for misinformation. Chris Campbell, executive director of the Boone History & Culture Center, explained the design of the exhibit in Nadja Sayej's article for the *Guardian*: "Half of the exhibit is devoted to the history of fake news, going back centuries, hoaxes and propaganda throughout the centuries. The second half is the antidote to fake news—truth, with proof, often black and white historical photos."

Biased in the Press

In their coverage of Cuba and the Spanish-American War, the Pulitzer and Hearst papers openly showed their bias against Spain. Since the establishment of professional journalism schools at the turn of the twentieth century, the ideal has been to strive for accurate, fair, and ethical reporting.

In a February 5–March 11, 2018, Gallup/ Knight Foundation survey, the organizations found that while Americans believed the majority of news reporting was accurate, they also believed the majority of the news they saw on television, read in newspapers, or heard on the radio was biased. In a press release sharing the survey's findings, the Knight Foundation reported:

To a large degree, bias and accuracy appear to be in the eye of the beholder, greatly influenced by whether one agrees with the ideological leaning of the news source. Americans' perceptions of fairly widespread bias and inaccuracy in news may be unduly influenced by the bias they perceive from the "other side" of the ideological spectrum rather than their own side.

Individuals and independent organizations have created lists and tools to help media consumers determine what biases do exist in the press. One example is patent attorney Vanessa Otero's MediaBiasChart.com, which measures the partisan bias and quality of the reporting offered by a number of print, television, radio, and internet news organizations. Another example is AllSides Bias Ratings, which uses its ratings system to classify news sources as leaning left, center, or right. "Left" refers to a liberal political view, "center" refers to an independent political view, and "right" refers to a conservative political point of view. Though bias does exist, not all press has the same bias. It is possible to find press coverage that confirms or challenges your own biases.

Aftermath of Fake News

The best and worst of today's journalism comes from this history. Joseph Pulitzer's legacy exemplifies both. His publishing empire grew by selling sensational stories. He also championed excellence

Associated Press photographer Liu Heung Shing and his colleagues received a Pulitzer Prize in 1992 for their coverage of an attempted coup in Russia.

in journalism. Pulitzer's will made provisions for the creation of the Pulitzer Prize, which recognizes achievement in journalism, letters, drama, and music. Journalism awards are presented in fourteen categories, which include investigative reporting, feature writing, editorial cartooning, and breaking news photography.

In his will, Joseph Pulitzer also bestowed Columbia University with a $2 million endowment for the establishment of a journalism school and for the creation of scholarships. Of this endowment, as reported on the official website for the prizes, Pulitzer said:

> *I am deeply interested in the progress and elevation of journalism, having spent my life in that profession, regarding it as a noble profession and one of unequaled importance for its influence upon the minds and morals of the people. I desire to assist in attracting to this profession young men of character and ability, also to help those already engaged in the profession to acquire the highest moral and intellectual training.*

The first classes at the Columbia Journalism School were held in 1912, four years after Walter

Williams started the School of Journalism at the University of Missouri. Williams, who served as the Missouri journalism school's founding dean, wrote the Journalist's Creed in 1914. It outlines eight beliefs for journalists to follow that profess the value of accuracy, fairness, and truth in journalism. The Missouri School of Journalism has Williams's creed on its website: "More than one century later, his declaration remains one of the clearest statements of the principles, values and standards of journalists throughout the world."

Coping with Fake News and Disinformation

Myths & FACTS

Myth: All members of the media are liberals.

Fact: More journalists identify themselves as independent rather than tied to one political party. While 28 percent of US journalists identify as Democrats and 7 percent as Republicans, 50 percent identify as independent, according to Tamar Wilner's January 2018 article for the Columbia Journalism Review.

Myth: No one reads newspapers anymore.

Fact: Whether in print or online, people continue to read newspapers. According to data released in Vividata's 2019 Winter Study, 74 percent of Canadian adults reported reading newspaper content the prior week, and 42 percent of newspaper readers reported they were exclusively print readers.

Myth: Fake news started because of social media.

Fact: Examples of deliberately false or exaggerated stories can be found throughout the history of print media. Social media, though, has made it easier for these stories to spread.

36

Faking the News

CHAPTER THREE

In the late nineteenth century, newspapers published fabricated or exaggerated stories to sell papers and influence the government to go to war. Contemporary reporters who have been caught writing faked stories or using questionable sources were driven by similar factors, from the pressure to succeed in a competitive industry to the desire to shine a spotlight on serious societal issues.

Whatever their intentions, the publication of these fabricated stories has consequences. Reporters and editors have lost their jobs. Newsroom practices are investigated and overhauled. Most damaging of all, the public can lose trust in the press after one of these stories is exposed.

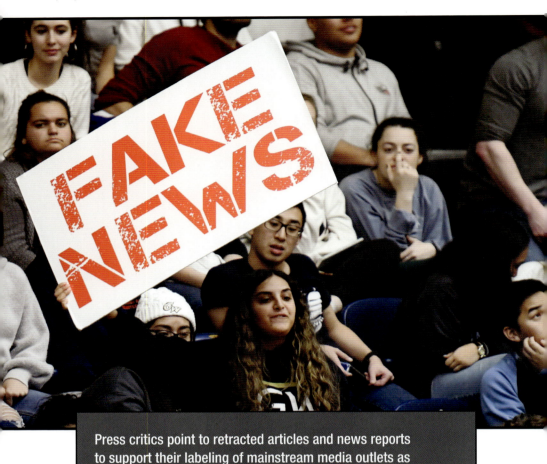

Press critics point to retracted articles and news reports to support their labeling of mainstream media outlets as "fake news."

Inventing a Boy

Heroin was becoming a major issue in Washington, DC, in the early 1980s. Reporters for the *Washington Post* were covering the crisis from a number of angles, including investigating the international drug trade and featuring community organizations assisting families dealing with addiction.

Janet Cooke was one of these reporters. Originally from the Midwest and boasting an impressive résumé that included a Vassar College education and fluency in several languages, Cooke was assigned by her editor to investigate a new type of heroin that ulcerated a user's skin. Though the young African American reporter was unable to track down the new drug, she was able to learn quite a bit about heroin abuse in Washington, DC, as later recounted in the April 19, 1981, article "The Players: It Wasn't a Game," written by *Washington Post* ombudsman Bill Green. Cooke also learned about children who were addicted to heroin.

From this investigation, the Pulitzer Prize–winning "Jimmy's World" was born. Published on the front page of the *Post* on Sunday, September 28, 1980, the article told the story of an eight-year-old heroin addict who lived with his addict mother, identified in the story as "Andrea," and her drug dealer boyfriend, identified in the story as "Ron." Cooke recounted the boy's ambition to become a dealer himself one day and graphically described how Jimmy would be injected with heroin by his mother's boyfriend:

Coping with Fake News and Disinformation

Washington Post reporter Janet Cooke returned her Pulitzer Prize when it was revealed that the article she wrote about an eight-year-old heroin addict was fabricated.

Ron comes back into the living room, syringe in hand, and calls the little boy over to his chair: "Let me see your arm."

He grabs Jimmy's left arm just above the elbow, his massive hand tightly encircling the child's small limb. The needle slides into the boy's soft skin like a straw pushed into the center of a freshly baked cake. Liquid ebbs out of the syringe, replaced by bright red blood. The blood is then reinjected into the child.

Jimmy has closed his eyes during the whole procedure, but now he opens them, looking quickly around the room. He climbs into a rocking chair and sits, his head dipping and snapping upright again, in what addicts call "the nod."

"Pretty soon, man," Ron says, "you got to learn how to do this for yourself."

Even as Cooke was working on the story, people in the newsroom had their doubts, as detailed in Green's article on "Jimmy's World," though concerns were not shared with top editors. Once the story was published, law enforcement and local officials challenged it. Police searched for the boy but could not find him. Members of the *Post* staff searched for him unsuccessfully. Cooke and her paper stood by the story. The *Post* was so confident in the story that it was submitted for a Pulitzer Prize.

Cooke was announced as the winner of the Pulitzer Prize for feature writing on April 13, 1981. Following this announcement, Jimmy's story started to unravel and, within two days of being awarded, Cooke returned the prize and the *Post* retracted the story.

Post ombudsman Green conducted an investigation of Cooke and "Jimmy's World" for his article "The Players: It Wasn't a Game." In it, he detailed Cooke's time at the *Post*, her construction of Jimmy's story, and how the story was revealed to be false.

Prior to joining the *Post*, Cooke was a reporter for the *Toledo Blade*. When she was announced as a Pulitzer Prize winner, writers at the *Blade* started putting together a story on their former employee. The paper referred to the official biography of Cooke released by the Pulitzer Prize committee and carried by the Associated Press wire service; the information in that biography did not match with the information the *Blade* had about Cooke, according to Green's reporting. The *Blade* contacted the Associated Press about the discrepancies and the Associated Press contacted the *Post*.

Over the course of several conversations with *Post* editors, Cooke revealed she had inflated her résumé and the biography she submitted with the Pulitzer Prize nomination. She also confessed that Jimmy did not exist. As Green recounted in his article, Cooke told David Maraniss, deputy managing editor, "There is no Jimmy and no family. It was a fabrication. I did so much work on it, but it's a composite. I want to give the prize back."

On April 16, 1981, the *Post* published an article by Maraniss, "The Post Reporter's Pulitzer Prize

Is Withdrawn," as well a message to readers, "The End of the 'Jimmy' Story." In it, the paper's editors apologized to their readers and reflected on what went wrong, concluding:

> *All this is an analysis, not an excuse. It seems to all of us around this newspaper that warning bells of some kind should have sounded, that procedures should exist, if they don't now, for smoking out a weird and atypical hoax of this kind. You may be plenty sure that there will be lots of self-examination, that the episode will be written about and explained in this paper and that more of the skepticism and heat that our colleagues traditionally bring to bear on the outside world will now be trained on our own interior workings. One of these episodes is one too many.*

In his analysis, Green found blame throughout the *Post's* newsroom, including the editors who did not challenge Cooke's reporting and the reporters who did not bring up their concerns about Cooke's story to management, each for their own varied reasons. Mike Sager, a *Post* reporter and colleague of Cooke's who also dated her, shared his own questions and conclusions from the "Jimmy's World" fallout, and its lasting impact, in a spring 2016 article for the *Columbia Journalism Review*:

> *The influence of Cooke's transgressions runs through the corpus of modern journalism like blood through the circulatory system, leaving no area untouched. Racial and sexual diversity in the newsroom. The use of unnamed sources. The responsibility of editors to question reporters' stories— should all writers be considered guilty until proven accurate? The responsibility of writers to fact-check their own stories. The pressures of working on deadline and being judged by one's output. The perils of literary journalism. And the perils of human frailty—what responsibility does an institution have to look beyond a person's résumé and into his or her psyche?*

Trusting a Source

In May 2014, the US Department of Education's Office for Civil Rights released a list of fifty-five colleges and universities being investigated for how they handled sexual violence and harassment complaints on their campuses. Not properly handling these cases could place schools in violation of Title

Corrections and Retractions

If a newspaper, magazine, website, radio, or television article has incorrect information, a correction or retraction will be issued by the editors to acknowledge the error. A correction details what error was made, like misspelling a source's name, providing the wrong date for an event, or attributing a quote to the wrong person. For newspapers and magazines, the correction will appear in a later issue, identifying the article title and publication date, listing and correcting the error, and apologizing to readers for the error being made. Online, articles are updated to reflect the correction and an editor's note will appear with the article to let readers know changes have been made. Television and radio news programs may have a regularly scheduled time slot for reporting their corrections.

Retractions are issued in serious cases, with the editors recalling the story. Retracted articles are sometimes removed from a publication's archives, as *Rolling Stone* did with "A Rape on Campus"—though the article can still be found via webpage archiving sites. If the article remains in the online archive, it will feature a note from the editors explaining that the story has been retracted, as is the case with the *Washington Post*'s online treatment of "Jimmy's World."

> *Rolling Stone* contributor Sabrina Rubin Erdely faced lawsuits for her article "A Rape on Campus," which featured allegations of a brutal sexual attack at a fraternity party.

IX, which, according to the Department of Education, "prohibits discrimination on the basis of sex in all education programs or activities that receive federal financial assistance."

One of the schools on that list was the University of Virginia (also known as UVA). When the list was published, a writer for *Rolling Stone* magazine was already working on an investigative feature about sexual violence on the campus and how campus administration dealt with those issues. In her reporting, writer Sabrina Rubin Erdely connected with a UVA staff member seeking a case to include in the article, as recounted in the article "Rolling Stone and UVA: The Columbia University Graduate School of Journalism Report: An Anatomy of a Journalistic Failure," which appeared in the December 4, 2014, issue of *Rolling Stone*. The staffer, a rape survivor who worked on campus as a sexual violence awareness specialist, knew a student on campus who might be willing to share her story.

Erdely first spoke with the student who would be known as "Jackie" in the article in July 2014—there were a total of eight interviews between July and October. Jackie described being assaulted at a fraternity party two years earlier by her date, an acquaintance, and several other unknown attackers. Those details became the focus of Erdely's article "A Rape on Campus: A Brutal Assault and Struggle for Justice at UVA," published in the November 19, 2014, issue of *Rolling Stone.*

Readers followed Jackie through the evening of the alleged attack, from her getting ready to be picked up by her date, who she only identified by first name to the writer, to her frantically calling her friends after her assault, who the writer did not interview. Erdely wrote:

> *When Jackie came to, she was alone. It was after 3 a.m. She painfully rose from the*

floor and ran shoeless from the room. She emerged to discover the Phi Psi party still surreally under way, but if anyone noticed the barefoot, disheveled girl hurrying down a side staircase, face beaten, dress spattered with blood, they said nothing. Disoriented, Jackie burst out a side door, realized she was lost, and dialed a friend, screaming, "Something bad happened. I need you to come and find me!"

The article followed Jackie as her friends tried to talk her out of filing charges, as she fell into depression, as she finally decided to go to campus administration with her story, and as she connected with a survivors' network on campus, naming the deans and advocates the anonymous Jackie met with. The article alleged that the university wasn't properly protecting students. Victims were encouraged not to press criminal charges and instead let the matter be handled within the school. If the school did find cause to punish a student for sexual assault, the punishments were not severe, according to the article.

Soon after Erdely's article was published, reporters from Slate and the *Washington Post* challenged its accuracy. The writer herself started having doubts about Jackie's story. *Rolling Stone* would retract the article and then enlist Steve Coll, dean of the Columbia School of Journalism, to conduct an investigation into what went wrong. "A Rape on Campus" no longer appears on the *Rolling Stone* website; "An Anatomy of a Journalistic Failure" has taken its place online. Erdely's original article can still be found online via web.archive.org. Of the

Rolling Stone enlisted Steve Coll, dean of the Columbia School of Journalism, to investigate the magazine's failings in the reporting of the retracted article "A Rape on Campus."

Columbia investigation, managing editor Will Dana recalled in part two of the 2017 HBO documentary *Rolling Stone: Stories from the Edge*:

> *We opened ourselves up to a very transparent investigation, and it wasn't seen as like, here's another otherwise trustworthy place that made a mistake, it was seen as OK, this is those elite mainstream media journalists revealing their true colors. People used to view* Rolling Stone *as being on their side, and something shifted more recently where, you know, it's just another piece of the mainstream media that couldn't be trusted.*

Coll and his collaborators on "An Anatomy of a Journalistic Failure," Sheila Coronel and Derek Kravitz, found:

> Rolling Stone's *repudiation of the main narrative in "A Rape on Campus" is a story of journalistic failure that was avoidable. The failure encompassed reporting, editing, editorial supervision and fact-checking. The magazine set aside or rationalized as unnecessary essential practices of reporting that, if pursued,*

would likely have led the magazine's editors to reconsider publishing Jackie's narrative so prominently, if at all. The published story glossed over the gaps in the magazine's reporting by using pseudonyms and by failing to state where important information had come from.

Phi Kappa Psi, the fraternity named as the location of the assault detailed in the *Rolling Stone* article "A Rape on Campus," was subjected to protests before the article's retraction.

The magazine also faced several lawsuits related to the article. Erdely was found responsible for defamation with actual malice against one of the deans named in the article, Nicole Eramo. *Rolling Stone* and parent company Wenner Media were also found responsible for defaming Eramo. The magazine reached a settlement with Phi Kappa Psi, the fraternity whose house was named in the article as the location of Jackie's assault, in its defamation case against *Rolling Stone*.

In concluding their report, the Columbia team emphasized the importance of the issues Erdely's article was meant to spotlight: "The responsibilities that universities have in preventing campus sexual assault—and the standards of performance they should be held to—are important matters of public interest. *Rolling Stone* was right to take them on. The pattern of its failure draws a map of how to do better."

Finding the Truth

CHAPTER FOUR

The articles "Jimmy's World" and "A Rape on Campus" were assigned to spotlight major societal issues. The reporters and editors behind both articles failed. Many other reporters and editors, however, continue to succeed by publishing well-reported, accurate articles about crime, corruption, and abuse.

Exposing Church Secrets

John J. Geoghan, a Catholic priest in Boston, abused children. The archdiocese of Boston knew, but instead of turning Geoghan over to the police when allegations were made—or when the priest himself admitted to abusing children—church leadership sent him for treatment and then reassigned him to new parishes. Members of these new parishes were told about the allegations made against Geoghan.

All of this was discovered by investigative reporters at the *Boston Globe*. The Spotlight Team, reporters Matt Carroll, Sacha Pfeiffer, and Michael Rezendes, and editor Walter V. Robinson spent months working on the first of its blockbuster articles about church leadership not only covering up abuse by priests but also allowing abusive priests to continue to work with children. Originally a two-part series, starting with "Church Allowed Abuse by Priest for Years" being published on January 6, 2002, and "Geoghan Preferred Preying on Poorer Children" published the following day, the team would go on to write six-hundred articles about abuse, cover up, and corruption in the archdiocese.

For the investigation, the reporters interviewed abuse survivors and reviewed court documents from civil cases that were filed against Geoghan. These included depositions and

Finding the Truth

Members of the 2003 Pulitzer Prize–winning *Boston Globe* Spotlight Team pose at the premier of the film based on their investigation into abuse in the Catholic Church.

personnel files for which the *Globe* had to file court motions to have made public. Church officials would not answer questions for these stories. According to their article in the *Globe*, the Spotlight Team explained:

> *In preparing this article, the* Globe *also sought interviews with many of the priests and bishops who had supervised Geoghan or worked with him. None of the bishops would comment. Of the priests, few would speak publicly. And one pastor hung up the phone and another slammed a door shut at the first mention of Geoghan's name.*

The Spotlight Team was awarded the 2003 Pulitzer Prize for public service for these articles. The story of the team's investigation of the archdiocese was dramatized in the 2015 film *Spotlight*. The church reached settlements with some survivors. Cardinal Bernard Law resigned his post heading the archdiocese, and the Vatican began hearing cases of bishops who had been accused of either abusing children or covering up that abuse. Members of the Spotlight Team, though, were hoping for more action from the church, as Michael Rezendes told Henry Barnes for an article in the *Guardian*:

It's been 13 years since we published our stories. So far, for survivors, there's been a tribunal that hasn't taken any concrete action. Over the last 10 years the Vatican has defrocked something like 850 priests and sanctioned maybe 2,500 more. But in terms of policy, there has been very little systemic change.

Taking On City Hall

In July 2010, reporters Jeff Gottlieb and Ruben Vives posed this question to readers of the *Los Angeles Times*, "Is a City Manager Worth $800,000?" By reviewing city documents obtained under the California Public Records Act, the reporters discovered the exorbitant salaries paid to officials in Bell, California, a city with a population of thirty-seven thousand that according to Gottlieb and Vives's article had a per capita income that was about half that for the United States.

The reporters shared salaries for the city's top officials, contrasting what those in Bell made with what their counterparts in other cities were paid. The reporters wrote, "In addition to the $787,637 salary of Chief Administrative Officer Robert Rizzo, Bell pays Police Chief Randy Adams $457,000 a year, about 50% more than Los Angeles Police Chief Charlie Beck or

Coping with Fake News and Disinformation

Los Angeles Times reporters Jeff Gottlieb (*left*) and Ruben Vives (*right*) celebrate their Pulitzer Prize win for coverage of government corruption in a small Southern California city.

Los Angeles County Sheriff Lee Baca and more than double New York City's police commissioner. Assistant City Manager Angela Spaccia makes $376,288 annually, more than most city managers."

The *Times* reports and state investigations revealed the level of corruption in Bell. City council members earned extra money by serving on agency

Making a Difference on Campus

As they were preparing an article on their new principal, six student reporters at Pittsburgh High School in Pittsburgh, Kansas, discovered some inconsistencies with the administrator's credentials. Through two interviews with the incoming principal, Amy Robertson, and three weeks of research, the reporters, who became known as the "Pitt 6"—Gina Mathew, Kali Poenitske, Maddie Baden, Trina Paul, Pat Sullivan, and Connor Balthozar—raised enough doubts about Robertson's qualifications that she resigned the principal position before she started.

The article, "District Hires New Principal," was printed in the *Booster Redux* on March 31, 2017, and provided details on Robertson's educational background. When interviewed by the students, Robertson said she had earned a bachelor of fine arts degree in theater from the University of Tulsa. The students contacted the University of Tulsa registrar's office and learned that the university never offered a bachelor of fine arts degree, only a bachelor of arts. The students also found that the university where Robertson received her master's and doctoral degrees was not accredited with the US Department of Education.

Of their discoveries, Balthozar is quoted in Samantha Schmidt's article for the *Washington Post* as saying: "All of this was completely overlooked. All of the shining reviews did not have these crucial pieces of information … you would expect your authority figures to find this." Four days after the article's publication, Robertson's resignation was announced at a school board meeting.

Staffers at the *Booster Redux* high school newspaper raised doubts about the qualifications of their school's incoming principal, reporting that led to her resignation.

boards that would meet for just one minute. Taxes were raised to cover the city manager's high salary. The city manager and other city officials would later be convicted of corruption. Gottlieb and Vives were awarded the 2011 Pulitzer Prize for public service for this coverage.

Reopening the Investigations

Robyn Doolittle, a reporter for the *Globe and Mail*, spent twenty months investigating how police departments across Canada handled sexual assault allegations for the February 2017 feature series "Unfounded: Why Police Dismiss 1 in 5 Sexual Assault Claims as Baseless." Doolittle shared with readers:

> *National policing data, compiled and reviewed by the* Globe *as part of its 20-month investigation, reveal that one of every five sexual-assault allegations in Canada is dismissed as baseless and thus unfounded. The result is a national unfounded rate of 19.39 per cent—nearly twice as high as it is for physical assault (10.84 per cent), and dramatically higher than that of other types of crime.*

For the nine articles that made up "Unfounded," the *Globe and Mail* reached out to every police service in Canada and requested data from their unfounded cases. The paper received data from 873 of the country's more than 1,100 jurisdictions. Fifty-four complainants were interviewed about their experiences of reporting a sexual assault. The investigation not only found that one in five sexual assault allegations were determined unfounded,

Globe and Mail reporter Robyn Doolittle's twenty months of investigation into police handling of sexual assault cases led to cases across Canada being reopened.

but that rates of unfounded cases varied drastically. Windsor, Ontario, for instance, had a 3 percent unfounded rate while Saint John, New Brunswick, had an unfounded rate of 51 percent.

Doolittle was honored at the National Newspaper Awards in 2018 with the prize for investigative journalism and was named journalist of the year. She was also awarded the 2018 Landsberg Award by the Canadian Journalism Foundation and Canadian Women's Foundation.

Following the release of "Unfounded," police services across the country reopened unfounded cases. As Doolittle told Jessica Howard for an interview that was posted on the Canadian Women's Foundation's website, that action by the police does not necessarily mean her investigation is over. She explains:

> *I think, from the* Globe's *perspective, we have to stay on top of the story. That's our role in this. A lot of promises were made after the Unfounded investigation [on the part of law enforcement, politicians, and government agencies], and we have to make sure that they're kept. The series launched in February 2017 and we went back before the end of the year and audited every police service in the country to see what they were*

doing: How many cases were they re-doing? How many cases had they recoded? Were they changing policies? Did they implement new training? We put all that information out there in the public for everyone to see, so that's our role.

Giving a Voice to the Victims

On August 4, 2016, the *Indianapolis Star* published "Out of Balance," an investigation that detailed how USA Gymnastics covered up sexual misconduct and abuse allegations against its coaches. That morning, "Out of Balance" reporters Marisa Kwiatkowski, Mark Alesia, and Tim Evans received an email that was later reported by CNN's Eric Levenson:

> *I recently read the article titled "Out of Balance" published by the IndyStar. My experience may not be relevant to your investigation, but I am emailing to report an incident that may be. I was not molested by my coach, but I was molested by Dr. Larry Nassar, the team doctor for USAG. I was fifteen years old, and it was under the guise of medical treatment for my back.*

Finding the Truth

Reporting in the *Indianapolis Star* helped lead to the conviction of former USA Gymnastics doctor Larry Nassar for sexual abuse.

That email was from Rachael Denhollander, who had filed a complaint against Nassar with Michigan State University Police shortly after contacting the *Indianapolis Star* reporters. She agreed to be interviewed and identified for a new article, "Former USA Gymnastics Doctor Accused

65

of Abuse," published in the paper in September 2016. The article alleged that USA Gymnastics knew about complaints against the doctor and did not adequately supervise him. That article now appears online with the following editor's note, "Since this article published, at least 150 people have come forward with allegations of sexual abuse against Dr. Larry Nassar. He was sentenced Jan. 24, 2018, to 175 years in prison after pleading guilty to sexually abusing seven girls."

At Nassar's sentencing trial, Michigan assistant attorney general Angela Povilaitis acknowledged the role the *Indianapolis Star*'s investigation played in the Nassar case, as reported by CNN's Eric Levenson:

> *It shouldn't take investigative journalists to expose predators. It should not take one brave woman put in the unenviable position and choice to go public with her name and be the only public person for months. But thank God we had these journalists. And that they exposed this truth and that they continued to cover this story.*

Information Overload

CHAPTER FIVE

The web is growing as a preferred source for news, the Pew Research Center has reported. In a December 2018 article, the center shared study findings revealing that of those Americans overall who preferred to read their news, 63 percent preferred to receive their news online, versus 17 percent who preferred print. Television is still the preferred platform for those who prefer watching their news—75 percent for TV versus 20 percent for web—though the web-watching number had grown by 12 percent above the rate reported by Pew in 2016. Age does make a difference in how people prefer to get their news, the center found. It reported: "Adults younger than fifty are more likely than those ages fifty and older to prefer the internet as the platform for getting news, regardless of which format (reading, watching or listening) they enjoy most." Seventy-six percent

A December 2018 Pew Research Center article reported that just 17 percent of American news readers prefer to get their news from newspapers, compared with 63 percent who prefer reading online.

of those under fifty who prefer to read their news selected the web as their preferred platform.

More of us are getting our news online, but the quality of the news we're finding may not be the best. A September 2018 Pew study found that of the Americans who get news at least occasionally on social media, 57 percent expect that the news will be largely inaccurate. This inaccurate news is being shared by some social media users. Released by ScienceAdvances in January 2019, the study "Less Than You Think: Prevalence and Predictors of Fake News Dissemination on Facebook" looked at the sharing of fake news articles around the 2016 US presidential election. It found:

Overall, sharing articles from fake news domains was a rare activity. We find some evidence that the most conservative users were more likely to share this content—the vast majority of which was pro-Trump in orientation—than were other Facebook users, although this is sensitive to coding and based on a small number of respondents. Our most robust finding is that the oldest Americans, especially those over 65, were more likely to share fake news to their Facebook friends. This is true even when holding other characteristics—including education, ideology, and partisanship— constant. No other demographic characteristic seems to have a consistent effect on sharing fake news, making our age finding that much more notable.

Even if shared in small numbers, misinformation and fake news can still have real consequences, as the people at the Comet Ping Pong pizza restaurant in Washington, DC, learned on December 14, 2016.

Victims of Fake News

Throughout her campaign for the presidency, Hillary Clinton faced criticism for her use of a private email server and potential mishandling of classified information during her time as secretary of state. She was also investigated by the FBI, with then agency-head James Comey recommending that no criminal charges be filed against Clinton in July 2016.

Three months later, while investigating a case involving the husband of one of Clinton's top aides, Comey announced the FBI would reopen its investigation into Clinton. On the evening of that announcement, according to a timeline researched by Amanda Robb (with additional reporting by Aaron Sankin, Laura Starecheki, Michael Corey, Jaime Longoria, and Japer Craven) for a November 2017 *Rolling Stone* article, a post was made on Facebook alleging that the presidential candidate, her husband, and several of their associates were involved in child abuse and trafficking. Similar

US presidential candidate Hillary Clinton was at the center of an internet conspiracy theory that alleged she, her husband, and their associates were involved in child abuse and trafficking.

posts appeared that day on message boards and in Facebook groups and were soon shared to Twitter.

The fake news story that became known as Pizzagate spread online over the course of five weeks. More fabricated and sensational details were added as the story spread. The narrative that eventually gained the attention of widely followed pundits like

An internet conspiracy theory alleging that children were being held captive in the basement of a pizza parlor led a gunman to open fire at Comet Ping Pong in December 2016.

Alex Jones of Infowars was that Clinton and her associates were trafficking and abusing children who were being held captive in the basement of Comet Ping Pong. A man from North Carolina, Edgar Maddison Welch, heard the story on one of Jones's broadcasts and, as Robb recounted in her article, felt compelled to take action:

Three days later, armed with an AR-15 semiautomatic rifle, a .38 handgun and a folding knife, he strolled into the restaurant and headed toward the back, where children were playing ping-pong. As waitstaff went table to table, whispering to customers to get out, Welch maneuvered into the restaurant's kitchen. He shot open a lock and found cooking supplies. He whipped open another door and found an employee bringing in fresh pizza dough. Welch did not find any captive children—Comet Ping Pong does not even have a basement—but he did prove, if there were any lingering doubts after the election, that fake news has real consequences.

Welch was sentenced to four years in prison and ordered to pay restitution for damage he did to the restaurant. No one at the restaurant was hurt in the incident. The Pizzagate conspiracy is still being spread online.

Funny, Not Fake

In addition to the fake news, scandals, rumors, and hoaxes trying to get our attention, humor and satire are also in the mix. Sometimes, these are confused

Gossip and Rumors

Fake news and disinformation are not limited to the online world. In our offline lives, we sometimes have to deal with false or exaggerated information in the form of rumors and gossip, sometimes as a participant and sometimes as a target. Rumors are the true, false, or exaggerated information that is spread, while gossip is the discussion of private information about another person that may or may not be true. Taking part in the spread of this kind of misinformation can bring people together. According to Jennifer King Lindley's article in *Real Simple*, Frank McAndrew, professor of psychology at Knox College in Galesburg, Illinois, shared, "Gossiping together strengthens bonds. It's a sign of trust: *I'm taking a risk you will not use this information in a way that will come back to haunt either of us.*"

There is good gossip, for instance, sharing positive and true information that a friend got into their dream college. Gossiping and spreading rumors can also be damaging, causing emotional and even physical distress to the person the rumors are about—and maybe the gossips, too. In Lindley's article, Erika Holiday, a Los Angeles–based psychologist, shared, "Emotional pain and physical pain are processed in

Information Overload

Fake news shows up in our everyday lives in the forms of rumor and gossip. Like fake news stories, rumors and gossip can have major consequences.

the same part of the brain. Gossip can hurt as much as being punched in the gut."

Just like fake news found online, hurtful rumors do not spread on their own. We can choose to help keep the misinformation moving or, if we know the information we are hearing is untrue or potentially harmful to another person, we can choose not to pass it along. As Moira Rose, Catherine O'Hara's character on *Schitt's Creek*, advised in the show's season four episode "Girls' Night" (which originally aired on January 30, 2018), "Gossip is the devil's telephone. Best to just hang up."

75

with real news. On television, *The Daily Show* has produced exaggerated, satirical segments that mimic actual news reports (and feature real people) while also commenting on true current events since its debut in 1996.

The Beaverton is a television show and website that features fictional stories that are inspired by news and current events in Canada. The show debuted in 2016, one day after the US presidential

The Beaverton is a television show and website that satirizes Canadian news and current events. Cast members of the show are pictured here.

election and six years after the website's launch. On television, segments have covered topics ranging from Canadian political figures to viral trends like the Tide Pod challenge to global conflict. Each is presented in the style of national evening broadcasts, but episodes are filled with exaggerated quotes and data. Online, *The Beaverton* covers the same topics as newspapers do, from national news to sports and culture. Their headlines include "Report: There Are a Bunch of Cities Outside Toronto with Their Own Streets and Buildings and Stuff," "Referee Reverses Call After Man Yells at TV Loud Enough," and "STUDY: TV Show Made for Teens Exclusively Consumed by Mid-Thirties Viewers."

Though aspects of its stories are false, the people behind *The Beaverton* show and website are quick to point out that what they produce is not fake news. Luke Gordon Field, who cofounded the website and is a cocreator, writer, and producer for the TV show, shared in an interview with Playback:

> *It was very interesting being in this place where we were doing this buzzword [fake news] that had come out, while at the same time doing what satire's job is, which is speaking the truth and take shots at the powerful. But at the same time we were also defending our own role in the world, because*

so many people who were mad about the role of fake news thought that applied to us. One of the more frustrating example of this was in TV panel discussions on the fake news phenomenon, where they would include the Onion *or* Beaverton *as examples of fake news, often with no distinction between satire and the Macedonian websites set up to fool people. Sometimes in comment threads you'll also see people write #fakenews or send us a Facebook message telling us we're fake news.*

The writers and editors behind the *Onion* have voiced similar frustration. Founded in 1988 as a print publication, the now web-only satirical publication features send-ups of current news and everyday life. Headlines have included "Exclusive TSA Pre-Check Allows Passengers to Fly Without Waiting for Airplane," "Dad Doesn't Trust the Fish Here," and "Trump Dismisses Trump as a Distraction."

Though created to be humorous and satirical, sometimes the *Onion*'s stories get taken seriously, like when a 2012 article naming North Korean dictator Kim Jong Un "Sexiest Man Alive" was picked up as real news by *China's People's Daily* in 2012. The *Onion*'s stories are not created to be taken

Information Overload

as fact, according to the people responsible for the site. Marnie Shure, an *Onion* writer, is quoted in Amanda Meade's article for the *Guardian Australia*:

> *The thing I like to emphasize is this: we work far too hard crafting our jokes for them to be taken as fact. If someone doesn't recognize the joke we're making, then that's a whole lot of labor lost. We aim never to trick people but rather to train them to see the world as we see it. In a world infested by "fake news," the intention [and subsequent execution] is everything.*

CHAPTER SIX

Consuming the News

Social media has helped bring the world together. It allows us to stay in touch with distant family and friends, build new communities around shared interests, and gain awareness of important issues. Social media, though, can also narrow our worlds, confining us to spaces where everyone we interact with shares our viewpoints and ideals.

In a February 2019 *Rolling Stone* article by Brian Hiatt, Twitter founder Jack Dorsey shared his concerns about this negative aspect of social media:

> *Like, we definitely help divide people. We definitely create isolation. We definitely make it easy for people to confirm their own bias. We've only given them one tool, which is follow an account that will 90 percent confirm whatever bias you have.*

Consuming the News

Social media has the power to unify and divide. While bringing us together with people who have shared interests, social media can also separate us from people with different viewpoints.

And it doesn't allow them to seek other perspectives. It contributes to tribalism. It contributes to nationalism.

Fake news and disinformation can thrive in this insular environment. For example, we may still share an inaccurate article if it confirms a belief we have. Treating articles like this with caution is one way to help ease the spread of fake news, according to Anthony Fargo, associate professor and director of the Center for International Media Law and Policy Studies at the Media School at Indiana University in Bloomington, Indiana. Fargo offered the following advice in a January 2019 email interview: "Be aware of where your news is coming from. If a claim appears too outlandish to be true or too convenient about confirming a bias you or other people may have, check to see if any other sources are also reporting it. If not, it's likely [made] up or embellished."

Addressing the Issue

News consumers have a responsibility in stopping the spread of fake news and disinformation. Social media companies are also stepping up and working on solutions for this issue. Facebook in particular has faced criticism for the way its platform has been used to spread inaccurate or fabricated information, especially in the aftermath of the 2016 US presidential election. The social media platform introduced a number of plans and initiatives with the goal of making it more difficult for disinformation to flow throughout its network.

In April 2017, Adam Mosseri, vice president of news feeds at Facebook, shared on the company's

Consuming the News

blog three key areas it would be addressing in its fight against what Facebook terms "false news." Those key areas include:

- Disrupting economic incentives, meaning to prevent posters from making money by spreading fake stories
- Building new products, meaning to develop or improve tools on the network to keep fake stories out of users' news feeds
- Helping people make more informed decisions, meaning to find ways to give users more information about the stories they're reading on Facebook

This plan is ongoing at the company and has been integrated into its community standards.

Informing and empowering users is an important part of Facebook's efforts. "The community is the best defense against misinformation in the long run and so by informing the community we can make that defense a little stronger," shares Dan Zigmond, director of analytics news feed, in the Facebook-produced 2018 short film, *Finding Facts: Facebook's Fight Against Misinformation.*

Company efforts like these spread to its other brands. In 2018, the Facebook-owned Instagram announced that it would be providing users with

83

Coping with Fake News and Disinformation

Distinguishing the Facts

Being a younger news consumer may mean you are better at determining facts versus opinions, the Pew Research Center discovered. In an October 2018 study for the center by Jeffrey Gottfried and Elizabeth Grieco, participants were asked to identify which five out of ten statements were factual and which five were opinions. Of the eighteen- to forty-nine-year-old participants, 32 percent correctly identified the factual statements, compared with 20 percent of those fifty and older. When it came to identifying the opinions, 44 percent of the younger participants were able to correctly identify all five opinion statements, compared with 26 percent of participants fifty and older. Being able to tell a fact from an opinion is an important skill for news consumers to have because it can help you gauge the bias and accuracy of an article you're reading. This skill can also be applied when doing research for schoolwork as you rate the value of the sources you plan to reference.

Consuming the News

more information about accounts with large audiences. This includes when the account started and where the account is based as a way for followers to check an account's legitimacy. The benefit to followers was explained by Instagram cofounder and chief technology officer Mike Krieger in Kaya Yurieff's CNN article:

Keeping people with bad intentions off our platform is incredibly important to me. That means trying to make sure the people you follow and the accounts you interact with are who they say they are, and stopping bad actors before they cause harm.

Getting the Facts

Verified facts are a powerful antidote to misinformation. Researching every questionable article that comes your way, though, would be timeconsuming and intensive. A number of individuals and organizations have stepped in to serve as fact-checkers for the internet, creating easily searchable sites web users can turn to when confronted with potentially false information, including those listed here.

Snopes (snopes.com) describes itself as "the internet's definitive fact-checking resource." Launched in 1994 to investigate urban legends, hoaxes, and folklore, the site has grown to research and validate a wide range of internet content, from political news to viral memes. Snopes details its fact-checking methodology online, which includes reviewing the claim in question with the original source and independent experts. All fact-checks are reviewed by at least one editor before being posted to Snopes.com. The website summarizes its work and process for readers as:

> *When misinformation obscures the truth and readers don't know what to trust, Snopes.com's fact checking and original, investigative reporting lights the way to evidence-based and contextualized analysis. We always document our sources so readers are empowered to do independent research and make up their own minds.*

PolitiFact (politifact.com) is a nonpartisan fact-checking organization owned by the nonprofit Poynter Institute for Media Studies that launched in 2007. The site checks specific statements made by politicians and notable figures for accuracy. It then uses its research—which includes on-the-record interviews and reviews of original documentation— to rate the statements on its Truth-O-Meter. The top rating a statement can receive from the site is

David Mikkelson launched the fact-checking resource Snopes in 1994. The site first investigated urban legends, hoaxes, and folklore, but now it covers a wide range of internet content.

"True," which the site describes as "accurate and there's nothing significant missing." PolitiFact.com's lowest rating is "Pants on Fire," which the site describes as "not accurate and makes a ridiculous claim."

PolitiFact.com highlights its independence online. It explains:

> *From the beginning, PolitiFact focused on looking at specific statements made by politicians and rating them for accuracy. PolitiFact is run by the editors and journalists who make up the PolitiFact team. No one tells us what to write about or how to rate statements. We do so independently, using our news judgment.*

The *Washington Post* originally launched its Fact Checker column in 2007 as part of

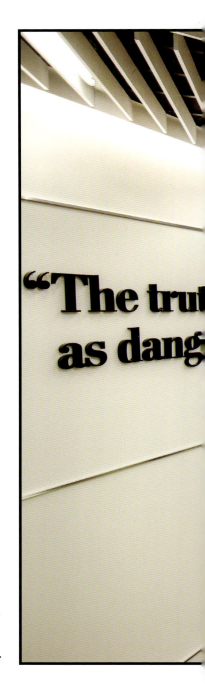

The *Washington Post*'s Fact-Checker column and web page rate the truthfulness of statements made by politicians and other notable public figures based on its "Pinocchio Test."

its coverage of the 2008 US presidential campaign. The column became a permanent feature for the paper in 2011. The Fact Checker (washingtonpost .com/news/fact-checker) focuses on newsworthy statements made by politicians, political candidates, diplomats, and interest groups. False statements are rated based on "The Pinocchio Test," named for the fairy tale character whose nose grew when he told a lie. "One Pinocchio" is given to statements that are mostly true; "Two Pinocchios" is for half-true statements; "Three Pinocchios" is for mostly false statements; and "Four Pinocchios" is for what the site describes as "whoppers." A "Bottomless Pinocchio" rating is given to statements previously rated with three or four Pinocchios that has been repeated at least twenty times. The Fact Checker describes itself as non-partisan, but acknowledges for readers the partisan nature of the statements it reviews, sharing:

We will strive to be dispassionate and non-partisan, drawing attention to inaccurate statements on both left and right. But we also fact check what matters—and what matters are people in power. When one political party controls the White House and both houses of Congress, it is only natural that the fact checks might appear too heavily focused on one side of the political spectrum.

(Divided government is much better for The Fact Checker.) We urge readers to bring to our attention possible false claims we might have missed.

FactsCan (factscan.ca) is a registered nonprofit organization that covers Canadian federal politics. Statements are rated on the site's five-point scale. True is the highest rating, awarded to statements found by the site to be verifiably accurate. Misleading statements are not false but may feature selective truth-telling or somewhat contradictory information. False statements are verifiably inaccurate. The Farcical rating is for statements that, according to the site, are "verifiably inaccurate and an egregious lapse of logic, almost indifferent to believability." If evidence cannot be found to validate or contradict a statement, the site gives it a Withholding Judgment rating. FactsCan describes its mission as follows:

To educate and engage Canadians in critical thinking and evidence-based political decision-making, to hold politicians accountable for their words, and to encourage honesty in political debate. The team does this through fact-checking claims made by federal politicians and other public figures. Fact checks separate the facts from spin, distortion, omission, error, and lies.

Becoming a Better News Consumer

Fact-checking sites are a quick resource for verifying if a story you have seen online is true. The web also offers tools to help you develop your own news judgment and become a smart consumer of information. Users are less likely to spread false, fabricated, or misleading information.

Sarah Blakeslee, a librarian with the Meriam Library at California State University, Chico, created the CRAAP Test in 2010 to help student researchers evaluate sources found online. The test can also be applied for judging the accuracy of news stories. CRAAP stands for currency (when the information was published), relevance (how the information

Consuming the News

Numerous tools and tactics are available to help you determine the validity of information you find online, from fact-checking websites like Snopes to evaluation methods like the CRAAP Test.

relates to your needs), authority (who the source is for this information), accuracy (that the information is valid and verifiable), and purpose (why the information is being shared).

In school, we learn about the Five Ws and One H—who, what, when, where, why, and how—as questions to consider in research projects. Journalists follow this pattern in their investigations, adding in a sixth W—who cares—to give their stories relevance for readers. These questions can also be helpful tools to use when evaluating the accuracy of the news you're reading.

In its "Authentication 101—Tip Sheet," MediaSmarts used the Five Ws to create questions to ask for help in recognizing false content online: "What kind of false content should I watch out for? Why is it being spread around? Who is spreading it? Do they have a good track record for accuracy? When did it start

Consuming the News

Attendees at the 2017 Kansas State Democratic convention show support for press freedom, which some fear is under threat as news outlets are labeled "fake news."

spreading? Where else can I find out is something is real?"

Think about questions you can ask when reading news stories that will help you judge the accuracy of the event or statements being covered. You might wonder who the source for this information is, what the point of view of the publisher is, when the events in the article happened, where else this event is being covered, why the story is being covered, how the publication learned about the events, and who cares that this event happened.

On the Media is a weekly radio program and podcast produced by public radio station WNYC. It investigates how the press covers major issues. On its September 20, 2013, episode, the program introduced the "Breaking News Consumer's Handbook." This resource offers news viewers, readers, and listeners, in the words of the program, "some tips for how, in the wake of a big, tragic story, you can sort good information from bad." The program released over twenty handbooks that offer advice on how to analyze and critique news coverage of topics, including election polls, protests, and storms.

Expanding the range of media you consume can also help you sharpen your news judgment. Scott Shane, investigative and national security reporter

Consuming the News

with the *New York Times*, offered this advice in an email interview on January 21, 2019:

> *Read/watch/listen to a wide variety of sources. If you love MSNBC, watch some Fox, and vice versa. If you are a conservative, read the opeds in the* NYT [New York Times]. *If you are a liberal, read the opeds in the* WSJ [Wall Street Journal]. *And whenever you see a story online—say being shared via Facebook—check the source. If you've never heard of it, there may be a reason. If it's shocking and inflammatory, and you haven't seen it reported elsewhere, it may well be fabricated.*

By building up your toolbox, sharpening your investigative skills, and developing some healthy skepticism, you can learn how to distinguish the real news from the fake, good information from bad, and help stop its spread.

Coping with Fake News and Disinformation

10 Great Questions to Ask to Become a Better Judge of News

1. Has the person who shared this article with you shared fake or misleading articles in the past?

2. Who wrote the article?

3. Where was the article originally published?

4. How reliable are the writer and publisher?

5. Is anyone else reporting this news?

6. Are there misspellings or other glaring errors in the article?

7. Who is quoted as a witness or expert in the article?

8. Are there photos, videos, or audio recordings to back this story up?

9. Does the article align too closely with your biases?

10. Do you feel confident sharing this article?

Glossary

archdiocese A territory overseen by an archbishop for the Catholic Church.

bias Favoring one side of an argument over another.

bipartisan The cooperation between two political parties that normally oppose each other.

censorship Preventing the publication or release of objectionable content.

complainant One who complains or makes the complaint in a legal action.

defrock To remove a priest from a position of honor.

fabricate To create false details or information that is presented as true.

fact An objectively verifiable piece of information.

freedom The ability to act without restrictions.

hoax A purposefully spread faked event or piece of information.

incite To stir up a person or organization.

journalism The act of providing a detailed, factual, objective description of an event.

libel A written defamatory statement.

liberty The freedom to do as you wish.

media The general term for print, audio, video, and web news and entertainment outlets.

objectivity Reporting on or analyzing an issue or piece of information without bias.

ombudsman A member of a newspaper staff who independently investigates issues at the publication brought up by editors or readers.

opinion A personal judgment or view on an issue or piece of information.

plagiarism Presenting someone else's work or ideas as your own.

press A general term for print, audio, video, and web news organizations.

privacy The ability to protect personal or sensitive information.

retraction The withdrawal of previously published content because of factual errors, plagiarism, or misleading statements.

right A legally protected act or action, such as voting.

satire The use of humor, irony, or exaggeration to make a point.

slander A spoken defamatory statement.

sources Individuals, reports, research, and other materials used for background in reporting a story.

ulcerate To be affected by or to develop similar symptoms to an ulcer.

For More Information

The Canadian Journalism Project (a project of Carleton University School of Journalism)

Room 4302C, River Building

1125 Colonel By Drive

Ottawa, ON K1S 5B6

Canada

(416) 979-5000, ext. 7433

Website: http://j-source.ca

Facebook and Twitter: @jsource

A collaboration of postsecondary journalism schools and programs in Canada, the donor-supported Canadian Journalism Project provides news, research, commentary, advice, and resources to journalism professionals, scholars, and students.

FactCheck.org

202 S. 36th Street

Philadelphia, PA 19104

Website: https://www.factcheck.org

Facebook: @factcheck.org

Twitter: @factcheckdotorg

FactCheck.org is a nonprofit, nonpartisan project of the Annenberg Public Policy Center of the University of Pennsylvania that monitors the accuracy of statements made by politicians in the United States, Canada, and around the world.

FactsCan

Website: http://factscan.ca

Facebook: @factscanada

Twitter: @factscan

FactsCan is a nonprofit, nonpartisan, and independent fact-checker of claims made by Canadian federal politicians and public figures.

NewseumED

555 Pennsylvania Avenue NW

Washington, DC 20001

Facebook and Twitter: @newseumed

The education branch of the Newseum, NewseumED provides educators and students with free First Amendment and media literacy resources online, as well as through classes held at the Newseum.

PolitiFact

c/o The Poynter Institute

801 Third Street South

St. Petersburg, FL 33701

(727) 821-9494

Website: https://www.politifact.com

Facebook and Twitter: @politifact

Owned by the Poynter Institute for Media Studies, the nonprofit PolitiFact rates the accuracy of statements made by US politicians, government agencies, political organizations, and more.

For More Information

Snopes

Website: https://www.snopes.com

Facebook and Twitter: @snopes

Snopes is an independent fact-checking publication that investigates folklore, urban legends, hoaxes, memes, rumors, and more found online.

Student Press Law Center (SPLC)

1608 Rhode Island Avenue NW, Suite 211

Washington, DC 20036

(202) 785-5450

Website: https://splc.org

Facebook: @studentpress

Instagram: @studentpresslawcenter

Twitter: @splc

The nonprofit, nonpartisan SPLC provides high school and college journalists, educators, and advisers with free legal information and free or low-cost educational materials.

For Further Reading

Fromm, Megan. *Accuracy in Media* (Media Literacy). New York, NY: Rosen Central, 2015.

Hall, Homer, Aaron Manfull, and Megan Fromm. *Student Journalism & Media Literacy.* New York, NY: Rosen Publishing, 2015.

Hand, Carol. *Everything You Need to Know About Fake News and Propaganda* (The Need to Know Library). New York, NY: Rosen Young Adult, 2018.

Leavitt, Amie Jane. *Digital Ethics: Safe and Legal Behavior Online* (Digital Citizenship and You). New York, NY: Rosen Young Adult, 2019.

Machajewski, Sarah. *American Freedoms: A Look at the First Amendment* (Our Bill of Rights). New York, NY: PowerKids Press, 2019.

New York Times Editorial Staff. *Cyberbullying: A Deadly Trend* (In the Headlines). New York, NY: The New York Times, 2019.

New York Times Editorial Staff. *Fake News: Read All About It* (In the Headlines). New York, NY: The New York Times, 2019.

New York Times Editorial Staff. *Hacking and Data Privacy: How Exposed Are We?* (Looking Forward). New York, NY: The New York Times, 2019.

New York Times Editorial Staff. *Identity Politics* (In the Headlines). New York, NY: The New York Times, 2019.

New York Times Editorial Staff. *Net Neutrality: Seeking a Free and Fair Internet* (Looking Forward). New York, NY: The New York Times, 2019.

Nieuwland, Jackson. *Coping with Social Media Anxiety* (Coping). New York, NY: Rosen Young Adult, 2018.

Bibliography

Booster Redux Staff. "District Hires New Principal." *Booster Redux*, June 14, 2017. https://www.boosterredux.com /news/2017/06/14/district-hires-new-principal.

Cooke, Janet. "Jimmy's World." *Washington Post*, September 28, 1980. https://www.washingtonpost.com/archive /politics/1980/09/28/jimmys-world/605f237a-7330 -4a69-8433-b6da4c519120/?utm_term=.5d69e7bf0339.

Coronel, Sheila, Steve Coll, and Derek Kravitz. "*Rolling Stone* and UVA: The Columbia University Graduate School of Journalism Report: An Anatomy of a Journalistic Failure." *Rolling Stone*, April 5, 2015. https://www.rollingstone .com/culture/culture-news/rolling-stone-and-uva-the -columbia-university-graduate-school-of-journalism -report-44930.

Doolittle, Robyn. "Unfounded: Why Police Dismiss 1 in 5 Sexual Assault Claims as Baseless." *Globe and Mail*, February 3, 2017. https://www.theglobeandmail.com /news/investigations/unfounded-sexual-assault-canada -main/article33891309/.

Erdely, Sabrina Rubin. "A Rape on Campus: A Brutal Assault and Struggle for Justice at UVA." *Rolling Stone*, November 19, 2014. http://web.archive.org/web/20141119200349 /http://www.rollingstone.com/culture/features/a-rape -on-campus-20141119.

Evans, Tim, Mark Alesia, and Marisa Kwiatkowski. "Former USA Gymnastics Doctor Accused of Abuse." *Indianapolis Star*, September 12, 2016. https://www.indystar.com /story/news/2016/09/12/former-usa-gymnastics-doctor -accused-Willabuse/89995734.

Follow Me. Directed by Asri Bendacha. Netflix, 2017.

Gottlieb, Jeff, and Ruben Vives. "Is a City Manager Worth $800,000?" *Los Angeles Times*, July 15, 2010. https://www.latimes.com/local/la-me-bell-salary-20100715-story.html.

Green, Bill. "The Players: It Wasn't a Game." *Washington Post*, April 19, 1981. https://www.washingtonpost.com/archive/politics/1981/04/19/the-players-it-wasnt-a-game/545f7157-5228-47b6-8959-fcfcfa8f08eb/?utm_term=.565f92c74d88.

Hiatt, Brian. "The Rolling Stone Interview: Twitter CEO Jack Dorsey." *Rolling Stone*, February 2019. https://www.rollingstone.com/culture/culture-features/twitter-ceo-jack-dorsey-rolling-stone-interview-782298.

Interview with Anthony Fargo. The Media School at Indiana University, Bloomington, Indiana, January 21, 2019.

Interview with Scott Shane. *New York Times*, Washington, DC, January 21, 2019.

Meade, Amanda. "The Onion in the Age of Trump: 'What We Do Becomes Essential When Its Targets Are This Clownish.'" *Guardian*, August 27, 2017. https://www.theguardian.com/culture/2017/aug/28/the-onion-in-the-age-of-trump-what-we-do-becomes-essential-when-its-targets-are-this-clownish.

Nobody Speak: Trials of the Free Press. Directed by Brian Knappenberger. Netflix, 2017.

Pfeiffer, Sacha. "Geoghan Preferred Preying on Poorer Children." *Boston Globe*, January 7, 2002. https://www.bostonglobe.com/news/special-reports/2002/01/07/geoghan-preferred-preying-poorer-children/69DE1kOuETjphwmIBcgzCM/story.html.

Bibliography

Phillips, Kyra. "CNN Special Report: Spreading Hate: The Dark Side of the Internet." CNN, May 5, 2018. https://www.cnn.com/videos/us/2018/05/02/csr-spreading-hate-ron-1.cnn.

Pinto, Jordan. "New Showrunners Talk TV: Jeff Detsky, Luke Gordon Field." Playback, March 2, 2017. http://playbackonline.ca/2017/03/02/new-showrunners-talk-tv-jeff-detsky-luke-gordon-field.

Rezendes, Michael. "Church Allowed Abuse by Priest for Years." *Boston Globe*, January 6, 2002. https://www.bostonglobe.com/news/special-reports/2002/01/06/church-allowed-abuse-priest-for-years/cSHfGkTIrAT25qKGvBuDNM/story.html.

Robb, Amanda. "Anatomy of a Fake News Scandal." *Rolling Stone*, November 16, 2017. https://www.rollingstone.com/politics/politics-news/anatomy-of-a-fake-news-scandal-125877.

Rolling Stone: Stories from the Edge 02. Directed by Alex Gibney. HBO, 2017.

Index

A
Alesia, Mark, 64
AllSides Bias Ratings, 32
Asaid, Deema Al, 6

B
Baden, Maddie, 59
Balthozar, Connor, 59, 60
Beaverton, The, 76–78
Bell, California,
    corruption in, 57–61
bias
    confirming one's own, 6,
        33, 80, 82
    in the press, 31–33, 84
Blakeslee, Sarah, 92
Bly, Nellie (Elizabeth
    Cochrane Seaman),
    22–23
Boone History & Culture
    Center, 29–31
Boston Globe, 54, 56

C
Campbell, Chris, 31
Carroll, Matt, 54
Catholic Church, 53–57
Clinton, Hillary, 70, 72

Coll, Steve, 49, 50
Comet Ping Pong, 70, 72,
    73
Comey, James, 70
Cooke, Janet, 39–44
corrections and
    retractions,
    explanations of, 45
CRAAP Test, 92–94
*Crown v. John Peter
    Zenger*, 15–17
Cuban independence,
    24–26

D
Daily Show, The, 76
Dana, Will, 50
Denhollander, Rachael, 65
Doolittle, Robyn, 61–64
Dorsey, Jack, 80–81

E
Erdely, Sabrina Rubin,
    46–52
Evans, Tim, 64

F
Facebook, 69, 70, 71, 78,
    82–85, 97

Fact Checker column (*Washington Post*), 88–91

fact checking organizations, 85–92

FactsCan, 91–92

fake news
history of, 28–31
how to spot, 92–97

Fargo, Anthony, 82

Field, Luke Gordon, 77–78

First Amendment, 11, 12, 13, 17, 19

"Former USA Gymnastics Doctor Accused of Abuse," 65–66

Freedom House, 21

G

Gardner, Victoria, 13–14

Geoghan, John J., 53–56

Globe and Mail, 61–64

gossip, 74–75

Gottlieb, Jeff, 57–61, 84

Green, Bill, 39, 41, 42, 43

Grieco, Elizabeth, 84

Gutenberg, Johannes, 7

H

Hazelwood School District v. Kuhlmeier, 11

Hearst, William Randolph, 23, 24, 25, 28, 31

Holiday, Erika, 74–75

I

Indianapolis Star, 64–66

Instagram, 83–85

J

"Jimmy's World," 39–44, 45, 53

Jones, Alex, 72

journalism schools, establishment of, 30, 31, 34–35

Journalist's Creed, 35

K

Knight Foundation, 32

Krauss, Clifford, 25

Krieger, Mike, 85

Kwiatkowski, Marisa, 64

L

Levenson, Eric, 64, 66

libel, 13, 14, 15, 16, 17, 21

Licensing Act, 10, 14

Los Angeles Times, 57–61

M

Maine, sinking of, 26

Maraniss, David, 42–43

Martin, Robert W. T., 14–15

Mathew, Gina, 59

McAndrew, Frank, 74

MediaBiasChart.com, 32

MediaSmarts, tips for spotting false content, 94–96

Mosseri, Adam, 82–83

N

Nassar, Larry, 64–66

New York Journal, 24

New York World, 22, 24

O

Onion, 78–79

Otero, Vanessa, 32

"Out of Balance," 64–66

P

Paul, Trina, 59

Pew Research Center, 67, 68, 84

Pfeiffer, Sacha, 54

Picciolini, Christian, 5

Pittsburgh High School (Kansas), 59–60

Pizzagate, 70–73

Poenitske, Kali, 59

PolitiFact, 86–88

Povilaitis, Angela, 66

presidential election (2016), 69, 75, 76–77, 82

press, the

bias in, 31–33, 84

in Canada, 19–21

in colonial America, 14–17

government regulation of, 9–14

in the nineteenth century, 22–24, 37

printing press, 7–9

prior restraint, 10

Pulitzer, Joseph, 22, 23, 24, 25, 28, 31, 33–34

Pulitzer Prize, 39, 41, 42, 56, 61

creation of, 34

R

"Rape on Campus, A," 45,

47–52, 53

Rezendes, Michael, 54, 56–57

Robb, Amanda, 70, 72

Robertson, Amy, 59, 60

Robinson, Walter V., 54

Robison, Jennifer, 19

Rolling Stone, 45, 46–52, 70, 80

rumors, 74–75

S

Sager, Mike, 43–44

satire, 73–79

Sedition Act, 16, 17

Shane, Scott, 96–97

Shure, Marnie, 79

slander, 17, 21

Snopes, 85–86

Soll, Jacob, 28–29

Spanish-American War, 26, 28, 31

Spotlight Team, 54–57

student press, freedom of, 11–13

Student Press Law Center, 12, 13

Sullivan, Pat, 59

T

Twitter, 71, 80

U

"Unfounded: Why Police Dismiss 1 in 5 Sexual Assault Claims as Baseless," 61–64

US Constitution, 7, 11, 13, 16, 17

V

Vives, Ruben, 57–61

W

Washington Post, 38–44, 45, 48, 60, 88

Welch, Edgar Maddison, 72–73

Williams, Walter, 34–35

Woolf, Christopher, 26

Y

yellow journalism/press, 24, 26, 28

Z

Zigmond, Dan, 83

About the Author

Devlin Smith has been writing about topics ranging from pop culture to small business to home décor for two decades. She got her first magazine subscription at age two and was inspired to study journalism by the writers whose bylines appeared in the magazines she read growing up. Smith earned a bachelor's degree in English with a journalism emphasis from Chapman University and has been proud to list her occupation as writer ever since. Today she works as a creative copywriter for the University of California, Riverside, where she writes for departments across campus, including the university's Ethnic & Gender Programs.

Photo Credits

Cover Anetlanda/Shutterstock.com; p. 5 OPOLJA/Shutterstock.com; p. 8 Heritage Images/Hulton Archive/Getty Images; pp. 12, 40, 46, 49, 51, 58 © AP Images; p. 16 © North Wind Picture Archives; p. 18 Yellow Dog Productions/The Image Bank/Getty Images; pp. 20–21 Kena Betancur/AFP/Getty Images; p. 23 Library of Congress Prints and Photographs; p. 24 ullstein bild Dtl./Getty Images; p. 27 Bettmann/Getty Images; p. 30 Universal History Archive/Universal Images Group/Getty Images; p. 33 South China Morning Post/Getty Images; p. 38 Mitchell Layton/Getty Images; pp. 54–55 George Pimentel/WireImage/Getty Images; p. 60 Keith Myers/TNS/Newscom; p. 62 David Cooper/Toronto Star/Getty Images; p. 65 Scott Olson/Getty Images; p. 68 Caiaimage/Paul Bradbury/Getty Images; p. 71 Joseph Sohm/Shutterstock.com; p. 72 The Washington Post/Getty Images; p. 75 Denis OREA/Shutterstock.com; p. 76 Andrew Francis Wallace/Toronto Star/Getty Images; p. 81 Monkey Business Images/Shutterstock.com; p. 87 Stephen Osman/Los Angeles Times/Getty Images; pp. 88–89 Nicole S Glass/Shutterstock.com; pp. 92–93 Rawpixel.com/Shutterstock.com; pp. 94–95 Mark Reinstein/Corbis Historical/Getty Images.

Design: Michael Moy; Layout and Photo Researcher: Ellina Litmanovich; Editor: Erin Staley